TEA

THE tea plant of today's commerce differs somewhat from that of a thousand years ago. This has been brought about by cultivation and experiments rather than by any change in climatic conditions. The tea-grower, having had sufficient proof of the hardihood of the native bush, began a series of experiments which have extended over hundreds of years until he has demonstrated that China, the legendary first home of the tea plant, must compete with other countries in producing this cheering household necessity.

The demand for different kinds of tea today has created many varieties, having a common origin, but manipulated so as to produce styles, flavors and other cup qualities distinct from each other, which have been grouped under different heads for commercial purposes.

The tea cut shown on the next page, illustrates the general appearance of the bush in its flowering stage, the leaves of which may be made up into any variety known to the tea drinking public.

TEA PLANT
REGISTERED.

A
Perfect
CUP OF TEA

ARTHUR GRAY, 1903
EDITED BY PAT ROSS

CHRONICLE BOOKS
SAN FRANCISCO

Copyright © 1995 by Pat Ross.

All rights reserved. No part of this book may be
reproduced without written permission from the Publisher.

Printed in Singapore.

Book and cover design by Sarah Bolles.

Library of Congress Cataloging-in-Publication Data available.

ISBN: 0-8118-0705-3

Distributed in Canada by Raincoast Books,
8680 Cambie Street, Vancouver, B.C. V6P 6M9

10 9 8 7 6 5 4 3 2 1

Chronicle Books
275 Fifth Street
San Francisco, CA 94103

*N*ewspaper writer, author, anthologist—Arthur Gray left a small but tidy legacy in several clever and erudite volumes expounding the details of daily living often taken for granted. His *The Little Tea Book,* now reissued in this edited version as *A Perfect Cup of Tea,* is possibly his most detailed and joyfully effusive contribution, published during a time of great flourish—America's Victorian era—when tea and good manners went hand in glove. Both were portentous to Gray.

Despite the lack of surviving biographical information about the man and his work, it's possible to piece together a few jigsaw details in an attempt to complete a mental puzzle of Arthur Gray. Born in Madison, Wisconsin, on May 26, 1859, Arthur Gray was educated in Madison's public school system. A bachelor until the age of thirty, Gray married a woman from Brooklyn, New York, named Ardelia. It appears that Arthur Gray then moved to Brooklyn, where he pursued his life's work as a newspaperman, editor, and anthologist. The news publications he worked for remain a mystery.

Happily, six congenial collections survive, providing glimpses into Gray the freelance writer/compiler. All of Gray's books revel in expressly intimate subjects that—both then and now—provide comfort and solace. Whether the subject is a cozy pair of slippers or a valued watch, a fancy dress coat or the importance of the chafing dish, Gray views each as essential to a cultivated society. In his own writing or through the excerpts he includes in his books, Gray has the ability to elevate something as elemental as the wearing of a bathrobe or the smoking of a good pipe to a fine art.

In a most dapper way and with a decidedly turn-of-the-century masculine bent, Gray speaks of those familiar and cherished moments, those pauses in one's day that take on special meanings for the event as much as the pause. His enthusiasm for the taking of tea—a civilizing tradition in any era—is unbounded. He is enthralled by its history, its soothing effects, its contribution to solitude and order. In just one small volume, Arthur Gray manages to dispense the entire tea heritage, ushering readers along at a breathless pace that never tires in its fascination with the subject.

At a dizzying stride, Gray finds just the right blend of poetry, essays, plays, and toasts, eager that the reader has not been cheated. Then, seemingly at random, he tosses in snippets of wit and wisdom—spoken by "authorities" ranging from an obscure English tea agent to the eminent Dr. Samuel Johnson. Although many of the selections by non-British sources seem influenced by British tradition in both spelling and syntax, the book was first published in America.

Several pages into my first reading of *The Little Tea Book,* I was compelled to search for my prettiest teapot and tea cozy, quickly rejecting the canister of prepackaged tea bags in favor of my sterling strainer and the special-occasion oolong leaves. Arthur Gray has a way of taking you back to a time when life was less hurried and tea sustained on many levels.

Pat Ross

MEETING AT BREAKFAST.

Thou soft, thou sober, sage, and venerable liquid! Thou innocent pretense for bringing the wicked of both sexes together in the morning! Thou female tongue-running, smile-soothing, heart-opening, wink-tipping cordial to whose glorious insipidity I can owe the happiest moments of my life.

Colby Cibber

"THE LITTLE ARMOUR BEARER"

*A*fter all, tea is the drink! Domestically and socially it is the beverage of the world. There may be those who will come forward with their figures to prove that other fruits of the soil—agriculturally and commercially—are more important. Perhaps they are right when quoting statistics. But what other product can compare with tea in the high regard in which it has always been held by writers whose standing in literature, and recognized for their good taste in other walks, cannot be questioned?

A glance through this book will show that the spirit of the tea beverage is one of peace, comfort, and refinement. As these qualities are all associated with the ways of women, it is to them, therefore—the real rulers of the world—that tea owes its prestige and vogue.

Further peeps through these pages prove this to be true; for nearly all the allusions and references to the beverage by male writers reveal the womanly influence that tea imparts. But this is not all. The sidelights of history, customs, manners, and modes of living which tea plays in the life of all nations will be found entertaining and instructive. Linked with the fine feminine atmosphere which pervades the drinking of the beverage everywhere, a leaf which can combine so much deserves, at least, a little human hearing for its long list of virtues; for its peaceful walks, talks, tales, tattles, frills, and fancies which go to make up this tribute to "the cup that cheers but not inebriates."

Arthur Gray

The
Origin
of Tea

Dharma, king of India, a religious high priest from Siaka coming to China to teach the way of happiness, lived a most austere life, passing his days in continual mortification and retiring by night to solitudes when he fed only upon the leaves of trees and other vegetable productions.

After several years passed in this manner, in fasting and watching, it happened that, contrary to his vows, the pious Dharma fell asleep! When he awoke, he was so much enraged at himself that, to prevent the offence to his vows for the future, he got rid of his eyelids and placed them on the ground. On the following day, returning to his accustomed devotions, he beheld with amazement two small shrubs of an unusual appearance springing up from his eyelids such as he had never before seen, and of whose qualities he was, of course, entirely ignorant.

The saint, however, not being wholly devoid of curiosity—or, perhaps, being unusually hungry—was prompted to eat of the leaves and immediately felt within him a wonderful elevation of mind and a vehement desire of divine contemplation with which he acquainted his disciples, who were eager to follow the example of their instructor. They readily received into common use the fragrant plant which has been the theme of so many poetical and literary pens in succeeding ages.

AN ANCIENT TALE

Legendary history informs us that DHARMA, son of KASI, a South Indian Prince and founder of the ZEN Sect of Buddhism, came to Southern China to introduce his doctrines.

Eventually he settled at Shorin-ji Temple on the famous Suzan mountain.

Here for nine years he sat outside of the temple in holy contemplation, denying himself food, drink and sleep, and even losing his legs from long disuse.

Once his eyes closed in sleep, which so angered him that he cut off both eyelids to prevent its recurrence, and, where he threw them on the ground, two tea bushes grew and flourished; and so tea originated.

Dharma died in 528 A.D. at an extreme age.

JAPAN GREEN TEA

Japan Green Tea is tea at its best, the NATURAL leaf, uncolored and unfermented, with all the fragrance of the fresh leaves preserved by immediate sterilization.

In the manufacturing process, the tea is prepared by means of the most modern scientific machinery, thus insuring the highest standard of purity.

The rich Vitamin C content is preserved because Japan Tea is NATURAL TEA UNFERMENTED. Fermentation destroys the valuable health element.

If interested in detailed information regarding the value of Japan Green Tea from the health standpoint, please write

American Japanese
Tea Committee
782 Wrigley Building,
Chicago, Ills.

Tea

by Francis Saltus Saltus

From what enchanted Eden came thy leaves
That hide such subtle spirits of perfume?
Did eyes preadamite first see the bloom,
Luscious nepenthe of the soul that grieves?

By thee the tired and torpid mind conceives
Fairer than roses brightening life's gloom,
Thy protean charm can every form assume
And turn December nights to April eves.

Thy amber-tinted drops bring back to me
Fantastic shapes of great Mongolian towers,
Emblazoned banners, and the booming gong;
I hear the sound of feast and revelry,
And smell, far sweeter than the sweetest flowers,
The kiosks of Peking, fragrant of Oolong!

WOOLSON SPICE CO'S,
Midsummer Greeting.

BUFFORD

*A*lthough the legend credits the pious East Indian with the discovery of tea, there is no evidence that India is really the birthplace of the plant. Since India has no record of date or facts, on stone or tablet, or has never handed down a single incident in song or story apart from the legend as to the origin of tea, one is loath to accept the claim, if claim they assert.

Certain it is that China, first in many things, knew tea as soon as any nation of the world. The early Chinese were not only more progressive than other peoples, but linked with their progress were important researches and invaluable discoveries which the civilized world long ago recognized. Then, why not add tea to the list?

At any rate, it is easy to believe that the Chinese were first in the tea fields and that, undoubtedly, the plant was a native of both China and Japan when it was slumbering on the slopes of India, unpicked, unsteeped, undrunk, unhonored, and unsung.

A celebrated Buddhist, St. Dengyo Daishai, is credited with having introduced tea into Japan from China as early as the fourth century. It is likely that he was the first to teach the Japanese the use of the herb, for it had long been a favorite beverage in the mountains of the Celestial Kingdom. The plant, however, is found in so many parts of Japan that there can be little doubt that it is indigenous there, as well.

The word *tea* is of Chinese origin, being derived from the Amoy and Swatow reading, *Tay,* of the same character, which expresses both the ancient name of tea, *T'su,* and the more modern one, *Cha.* Japanese tea, *Chiya,* is pronounced *Châ.*

Tea was not known in China before the Tang dynasty, 618–96 A.D. An infusion of some kind of leaf, however, was used as early as the Chow dynasty, 1122–255 B.C., as we learn from the *Urh-ya,* a glossary of terms used in ancient history and poetry. This work, which is classified by subjects, has been assigned at the beginning of the Chow dynasty, but belongs more properly to the era of Confucius, K'ung Kai, 551–479 B.C.

INTRODUCTION OF TEA INTO JAPAN

The tea plant is native to Japan according to the earliest recorded history, but, in 805 A.D., the China tea plant was also brought over to Japan. The two varieties were gradually merged into one. In the earlier part of the 13th century, tea was cultivated quite extensively, and soon became a national favorite.

For more than a thousand years, the tea plantations have been as much a part of the life and color of old Japan as the blossom-laden cherry trees or the snow-capped Mount Fuji.

ORIGIN OF TEA

It is definitely known that tea was used in China early in the 6th century. In many parts of the country, especially in the interior, people suffered from disorders due to drinking impure water. Soon they learned to boil it, and gradually added herbs to give flavor to the drink. It was found that tea when so applied was palatable and sustaining; and, as the use of it grew, means were discovered for preparing the leaf so that it could be kept and used all the year round.

Although known in Japan for more than a thousand years, tea only gradually became the national beverage as late as the fourteenth century. In the first half of the eighth century, 729 A.D., there was a record made of a religious festival at which the forty-fifth mikado—*Shommei Tenno*, or "Sublime Gate"—entertained the Buddhist priests with tea, a hitherto unknown beverage from Korea, which was for many years the high road of Chinese culture to Japan.

After the ninth century, and for four centuries thereafter, tea fell into disuse and almost oblivion among the Japanese. The nobility and Buddhist priests, however, continued to drink it as a luxury.

GOVERNMENT PROTECTION

All Tea entering the United States is carefully tested for purity by Government Tea Examiners, stationed at the principal ports. Tea of inferior quality is refused entry.

When, twenty years ago, the United States prohibited the importation of artificially colored tea, the Japanese Government promptly cooperated by stopping its manufacture.

Japan Green Tea is dependable for purity.

HERE SCIENCE ENTERS

Dr. Miura, an eminent Japanese scientist, after years of careful experimental work, definitely established that Japan Green Tea is rich in an important element—Vitamin C—vitally necessary for perfect health. His discovery was carefully checked for many months at a leading American University and fully corroborated in every respect.

For many years, Japan Green Tea has been one of the most popular Teas in the United States, winning favor on the merit of its delicate, delicious flavor, which caused it to be called the Champagne of Teas. Now a highly important health asset is recognized in connection with its daily use, and aside from its delicious beverage qualities, it is especially recommended as a great aid in maintaining the body in a sound and fit condition. Japan Tea rejuvenates and furnishes vigor and resistance.

During the reign of the eighty-third emperor, 1199–1210 A.D., the cultivation of tea was permanently established in Japan. In 1200, the bonze, Yei-Sei, brought tea seeds from China, which he planted on the mountains in one of the most northern provinces. Yei-Sei is also credited with introducing the Chinese custom of ceremonious tea drinking. At any rate, he presented tea seeds to Mei-ki, the abbot of the monastery of To-gano (to whom the use of tea had been recommended for its stimulating properties), and instructed him in the mystery of its cultivation, treatment, and preparation. Mei-ki, who laid out plantations near Uzi, was successful as a pupil. And even now the tea growers of that neighborhood pay tribute to his memory annually by offering at his shrine the first gathered tea leaves. After that period, the use of tea became more and more in fashion, the monks and their kindred having discovered its property of keeping them awake during long vigils and nocturnal prayers.

From this time on, the development and progress of the plant are interwoven with the histories and customs of these countries.

▬▶ Tea Terms ◀▬

Japanese		*Chinese*	
Ori-mono-châ	Folded Tea	Bohea	Happy Establishment
Giy-oku-ro-châ	Dew Drop Tea	*So called after two ranges of hills, Fu-Kien or Fo-Kien.*	
Usu-châ	Light Tea	Congou	Labor
Koi-châ	Dark Tea	*Named so at Amoy from the labor in preparing it.*	
To-bi-dashi-châ	Sifted Tea	Sou chong	Small Kind
Ban-châ	Common Tea	Hyson	Flourishing Spring
Yu-Shiyutsu-châ	Export Tea	Pe-koe	White Hair
Neri-châ	Brick Tea	*So called because only the youngest leaves are*	
Koku-châ	Black Tea	*gathered, which still have the delicate*	
Ko-châ	Tea Dust Broken Leaves	*down—white hair on the surface.*	
Riyoku-châ	Green Tea	Pou-chone	Folded Tea
		So called at Canton after the manner of picking it.	

*P*repared in Central China from the commonest sorts of tea, by soaking the tea refuse, such as broken leaves, twigs, and dust, in boiling water and then pressing them into molds. Used in Siberia and Mongolia, where it also serves as a medium of exchange. When testing the quality, the Mongols place the bricks on the head and try to pull downward over the eyes. They reject the brick as worthless if it breaks or bends.

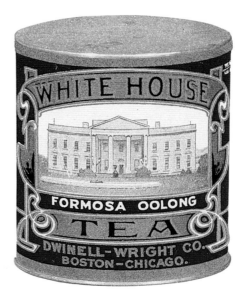

LINHERR & CO.'S HAIR TEA SET, AT CRYSTAL PALACE.

Earliest Mention of Tea

The first mention of tea by an Englishman is to be found in a letter from Mr. Wickham, an agent of the East India Company, written from Japan on the 27th of June, 1615, to Mr. Eaton, another officer of the company and a resident of Macao, asking him to send "a pot of the best chaw." In Mr. Eaton's accounts of expenditure occurs this item:

"Three silver porringiys to drink chaw in."

On Tea

The following short poem by Edmund Waller is believed to be the first one written in praise of the "cup that does not inebriate":

Venus her myrtle, Phoebus has her bays;
Tea both excels, which she vouchsafes to praise.
The best of Queens, and best of herbs, we owe
To that bold nation, which the way did show
To the fair region where the sun doth rise,
Whose rich productions we so justly prize.
The Muse's friend, tea does our fancy aid,
Repress those vapors which the head invade,
And keep the palace of the soul serene,
Fit on her birthday to salute the Queen.

Waller was born in 1605 and died in 1687.

Tea
Kettle

CELTIC

Tea was brought into Europe by the Dutch East India Company in 1610. It was at least forty, and perhaps forty-seven, years later that England woke up to the fascination of the new drink. Dr. Johnson puts it at even a later date, for he claims that tea was first introduced into England by Lords Arlington and Ossory in 1666, and really made its debut into society when the wives of these noblemen gave it its vogue.

If Dr. Johnson's statement is intended to mean that nothing is anything until the red seal of the select says, "Thus shall it be," he is right in the year he has selected. If, on the other hand, the Doctor had in mind society at large, he is "mixed in his dates" or leaves, for tea was drawn and drunk in London nine years before that date.

Garway, the founder of Garraway's coffee house, claimed the honor of being first to offer tea in leaf and drink for public sale in 1657. It is pretty safe to fix the entrance of tea into Europe even a few years ahead of his announcement, for merchants in those days did not advertise their wares in advance.

However, this date is about the beginning of tea time, for in the *Mercurius Politicius* of September 1658 appeared the following advertisement:

That excellent and by all Physitians
approved China drink, called by the Chinese,
Tcha, by other nations, Tay or Tea, is sold at the
Sultana's Head, a Copphee House, in Sweetings
Rents, by the Royal Exchange, London.

Like all new things when they have fastened on to the public's
favor, tea was on everybody's lips and in everybody's mouth. It was lauded
to the skies and was supposed to be good for all the ills of the flesh. It would
cure colds and consumption, clear the sight, remove lassitude, purify the
liver, improve digestion, create appetite, strengthen the memory, and cure
fever and ague.

One panegyrist says, while never putting the patient in mind of
his disease, it cheers the heart without disordering the head; strengthens
the feet of the old, and settles the heads of the young; cools the brain of the
hard drinker, and warms that of the sober student; relieves the sick, and
makes the healthy better. Epicures drink it for want of an appetite; bon
vivants to remove the effects of a surfeit of wine; gluttons as a remedy for

indigestion; politicians for the vertigo; doctors for drowsiness; prudes for the vapors; wits for the spleen; and beaux to improve their complexions. Summing up, he declares tea to be a treat for the frugal, a regale for the luxurious, a successful agent for the man of business, and a bracer for the idle.

Poets and verse makers joined the chorus in praise of tea in both Greek and Latin. One poet pictures Hebe pouring the delightful cup for the goddesses who, finding it made their beauty brighter and their wit more brilliant, drank so deeply as to disgust Jupiter, who had forgotten that he, himself,

Drank tea that happy morn,
When wise Minerva of his brain was born.

Laureant Tate, who wrote a poem on tea in two cantos, described a family jar among the fair deities because each desired to become the special patroness of the ethereal drink destined to triumph over wine. Another versifier exalts it at the expense of its would-be rival, coffee:

> In vain would coffee boast an equal good,
> The crystal stream transcends the flowing mud
> Tea, even the ills from coffee spring repairs,
> Disclaims its vices and its virtues shares.

Another despairing enthusiast exclaims:

> Hail, goddess of the vegetable, hail!
> To sing thy worth, all words, all numbers, fail!

The new beverage did not have the field all to itself, however. For, while it was generally admitted that:

> Tea was fixed, and come to stay,
> It could not drive good meat and drink away.

Lovers of the old and conservative customs of the table were not anxious to try the novelty. Others shied at it; some flirted with it in tiny teaspoonfuls; others openly defied and attacked it. Among the latter were a number of robust versifiers and physicians.

> 'Twas better for each British virgin,
> When on roast beef, strong beer and sturgeon,
> Joyous to breakfast they sat round,
> Nor were ashamed to eat a pound.

The fleshly school of doctors were only too happy to disagree with their brethren respecting the merits and demerits of the newfangled drink; and it is hard to say which were most bitter, the friends or the foes of tea.

Maria Theresa's physician, Count Belchigen, attributed the discovery of a number of new diseases to the debility born of daily tea drinking. Dr. Paulli denied that tea had either taste or fragrance, owing its reputation entirely to the peculiar vessels and water used by the Chinese. Thus it was folly to partake of it, unless tea drinkers could supply themselves with pure water from the Vassie and the fragrant teapots of Gnihing. This sagacious

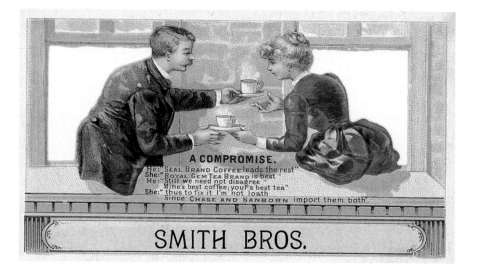

A COMPROMISE.

He: "SEAL BRAND COFFEE leads the rest"
She: "ROYAL GEM TEA BRAND is best"
He: "Still we need not disagree"
Mine's best coffee; your's best tea"
She: "thus to fix it I'm not loath
Since CHASE AND SANBORN import them both".

SMITH BROS.

sophist and dogmatizer also discovered that, among other evils, tea drinking deprived its devotees of the power of expectoration and entailed sterility. Therefore he hoped Europeans would thereafter keep to their natural beverages—wine and ale—and reject coffee, chocolate, and tea, which were all equally bad for them.

In spite of the array of old-fashioned doctors, wits, and lovers of the pipe and bottle who opposed evil effects, sneered at the finely bred men of

England being turned into women, and grumbled at the stingy custom of calling for dishwater after dinner, the custom of tea drinking continued to grow. By 1689 the sale of the leaf had increased sufficiently to make it politic to reduce the duty on it from eight pence on the decoction to five shillings a pound on the leaf. The value of tea at this time may be estimated from a

customhouse report of the sale of a quantity of divers sorts and qualities, the worst being equal to that "used in coffee houses for making single tea," which being disposed of by "inch of candle," fetched an average of twelve shillings a pound.

During the next three years the consumption of tea was greatly increased; but very little seems to have been known about it by those who drank it—if we may judge from the enlightenment received from a pamphlet, given gratis, "up one flight of stairs, at the sign of the Anodyne Necklace, without Temple Bar." All it tells us about tea is that it is the leaf of a little shoot growing plentifully in the East Indies; that Bohea—called by the French "Bean Tea"—is best of a morning with bread and butter, being of a more nourishing nature than the green, which may be used when a meal is not wanted. Three or four cups at a sitting are enough; and a little milk or cream renders the beverage smoother and more powerful in blunting the acid humors of the stomach.

The satirists believed that tea had a contrary effect upon the acid humors of the mind, making the tea table the arena for the display of the feminine capacity for backbiting and scandal. Listen to Swift describe a lady enjoying her evening cups of tea:

> Surrounded with the noisy clans
> Of prudes, coquettes and harridans.
> Now voices over voices rise,
> While each to be the loudest vies;
> They contradict, affirm, dispute,
> No single tongue one moment mute;
> All mad to speak, and none to hearken,
> They set the very lapdog barking;
> Their chattering makes a louder din
> Than fish-wives o'er a cup of gin;
> Far less the rabble roar and rail
> When drunk with sour election ale.

Sturges' Electro Plated Tea Kettle and Stand.

"School or college friends form desirable elements for a successful house party."

Even gentle Gay associated soft tea with the temper of women when he pictures Doris and Melanthe abusing all their bosom friends, while

Through all the room
From flowery tea exhales a fragrant fume.

But not all the women were tea drinkers in those days. There was Madam Drake, the proprietress of one of the three private carriages Manchester could boast. Few men were as courageous as she in declaring against the tea table when they were but invited guests. Madam Drake did not hesitate to make it known when she paid an afternoon's visit that she expected to be offered her customary solace—a tankard of ale and a pipe of tobacco.

Another female opponent of tea was the *Female Spectator,* which declared the use of the fluid to be not only expensive, but pernicious; the utter destruction of all economy, the bane of good housewifery, and the source of all idleness. Trades-men especially suffered from the habit. They could not serve their customers because their apprentices were absent during the busiest hours of the day drumming up gossips for their mistresses' tea tables.

This same censor says that the most temperate find themselves obliged to drink wine freely after tea, or supplement their Bohea with rum and brandy, the bottle and glass becoming as necessary to the tea table as the slop basin.

Although Jollas Hanway, the father of the umbrella, was successful in keeping off water, he was not successful in keeping out tea. All he did accomplish in his essay on the subject was to call forth a reply from Dr. Johnson who, strange to say, instead of vigorously defending his favorite tipple, rather

excuses it as an amiable weakness . . . confessing that tea is a barren super-
fluity, fit only to amuse the idle, relax the studious, and dilute the meals of
those who cannot take exercise and will not practice abstinence. His chief
argument in tea's favor is that it is drunk in no great quantity even by those
who use it most, and as it neither exhilarates the heart nor stimulates the
palate is, after all, but a nominal entertainment, serving as a pretence for
assembling people together, for interrupting business, and diversifying idleness. He did admit that, perhaps, while gratifying the taste without nourishing the body, it is quite unsuited to the lower classes.

It is a singular fact, too, that at that period there was no other really vigorous defender of the beverage. All the best of the other writers did was to praise its pleasing qualities, associations, and social attributes.

Still, tea grew in popular favor, privately and publicly. The custom had now become so general that every wife looked upon the teapot, cups, and caddy to be as much her right by marriage as the wedding ring itself. Fine ladies enjoyed the crowded public entertainments with tea below stairs and ventilators above. Citizens, fortunate enough to have leaden roofs to their houses, took their tea and their ease thereon. On Sundays, finding the country lanes leading to Kensington, Hampstead, Highgate, Islington, and Stepney "to be much pleasanter than the paths of the gospel," the people flocked to those suburban resorts with their wives and children to take tea under the trees. In one of Coleman's plays, a Spitalfield's dame defines the acme of elegance as

> **Drinking tea on summer afternoons**
> **At Bagnigge Wells with china and gilt spoons.**

London was surrounded with tea gardens, the most popular being Sadler's Wells, Merlin's Cave, Cromwell Gardens, Jenny's Whim, Cuper Gardens, London Spa, and the White Conduit House, where they used to take in fifty pounds on a Sunday afternoon for sixpenny tea tickets.

One D'Archenholz was surprised by the elegance, beauty, and luxury of these resorts where, Steele said, they swallowed gallons of the juice of tea, while their own dock leaves were trodden underfoot.

The ending of the East India Company's monopoly of the trade, coupled with the fact that the legislature recognized that tea had passed out of the catalogue of luxuries into that of necessities, began a new era for the queen of drinks destined to reign over all other beverages.

Vol. LI. No. 1326   MARCH 26, 1908   PRICE, 10 CENTS

LIFE

HENRY · HUTT

PRUDENTIAL COOK BOOK

FIRST AID
HINTS
~
CARE OF THE
BABY

W. MEYNER

*Dr. Samuel Johnson drew
his own portrait thus:*

"*A hardened and shameless tea-drinker,
who for twenty years diluted his meals with the infusion
of this fascinating plant; whose kettle had scarcely time
to cool; who with tea amused the evening, with tea solaced
the midnight, and with tea welcomed the morning.*"

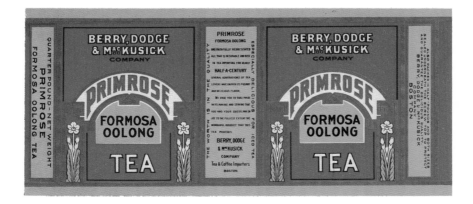

In the drama of the past
Thou art featured in the cast;
(O Tea!)
And thou hast played thy part
With never a change of heart
(O Tea!)
For 'mid all the ding and dong
Waits a welcome—soothing song,
For fragrant Hyson and Oolong.

A song of peace, through all the years,
Of fireside fancies, devoid of fears,
Of mothers' talks and mothers' lays
Of grandmothers' comforts—quiet ways.
Of gossip, perhaps—still and yet—
What of Johnson? Would we forget
The pictured cup; those merry times,
When round the board, with ready rhymes
Waller, Dryden, and Addison-Young,
Grave Pope to Gay, when Cowper sung?
Sydney Smith, too; gentle Lamb brew,
Tennyson, Dickens, Doctor Holmes knew,
The cup that cheered, those sober souls,
Tiny tea-trays, samovars, and bowls.

So here's a toast to the queen of plants,
The queen of plants—Bohea!
Good wife, ring for your maiden aunts,
We'll all have cup of tea.

Arthur Gray

Tea Leaves

by John Ernest McCann

According to Henry Thomas Buckle, the author of *The History of Civilization in England,* who was the master of eighteen languages, had a library of 22,000 volumes and an income of $75,000 a year, at the age of twenty-nine (he died in 1860, at the age of thirty-nine), tea making and drinking were, or are, what Wendell Phillips would call lost arts. He thought that when it came to brewing tea, the Chinese philosophers were not living in his vicinity. He wrote that until he showed her how, no woman of his acquaintance could make a decent cup of tea. He insisted upon a warm cup, and even spoon and saucer. Not that Mr. Buckle ever sipped tea from a saucer. Of course, he was right in insisting upon those above-mentioned things, for tea things, like a tea party, should be in sympathy with the tea, not antagonistic to it. Still, not always; for on one memorable occasion in the little town of Boston, the greatest tea party in history was anything but sympathetic. But let that pass.

Emperor Kien Lung wrote for the benefit of his children, just before he left the Flowery Kingdom for a flowerier:

> **Set a teapot over a slow fire; fill it with cold water; boil it long enough to turn a lobster red; pour it on the quantity of tea in a porcelain vessel; allow it to remain on the leaves until the vapor evaporates, then sip it slowly, and all your sorrows will follow the vapor.**

He says nothing about milk or sugar. But, to me, tea without sugar is poison, as it is with milk. I can drink one cup of tea or coffee with sugar, but without milk, and feel no ill effects; but if I put milk in either tea or coffee, I am as sick as a defeated candidate for the presidency. That little bit of fact is written as a hint to many who are ill without knowing why they are, after drinking tea, or coffee, with milk in it. I don't think that milk was ever intended for coffee or tea. Why should it be? Who was the first to color tea and coffee with milk? It may have been a mad prince, in the presence of his flatterers and imitators, to be odd; or just to see if his flatterers would adopt the act.

The Russians sometimes put champagne in their tea; the Germans, beer; the Irish, whiskey; the New Yorker, ice cream; the English, oysters or clams, if in season; the true Bostonian, rose leaves; and the Italian and Spaniard, onions and garlic.

You all know one of the following lines, imperfectly. Scarcely one in one hundred quotes them correctly. I never have quoted them as written, offhand—but lines run out of my head like schoolboys out of school,

> **When the lessons and tasks are all ended**
> **And school for the day is dismissed.**

Here are the lines:

> **Now stir the fire, and close the shutters fast;**
> **Let fall the curtains; wheel the sofa round;**
> **And while the bubbling and loud-hissing urn**
> **Throws up a steamy column, and the cups**
> **That cheer, but not inebriate, wait on each,**
> **To let us welcome peaceful evening in.**

Isn't that a picture? Not one superfluous word in it! Who knows its author, or when it was written, or can quote the line before or after

> **the cups**
> **that cheer, but not inebriate?**

or in what poem the lines run down the ages? I tell you. Not I. I don't believe in encouraging laziness. If I tell you, you will let it slip from your memory, like a panic-stricken eel through the fingers of a panic-stricken schoolboy; but if you hunt it up, it will be riveted to your memory, like a bullet, and one never forgets when, where, how, why, and from whom he receives that.

What a pity that, in Shakespeare's time, there was no tea table! What a delightful comedy he could, and would, have written around it, placing the scene in his native Stratford! What a charming hostess at a tea table his mother, Mary Arden (loveliest of womanly names), would have made! Any of the ladies of the delightful

"Cranford" wouldn't be a circumstance to a tea table scene in a Warwickshire comedy with lovely Mary Arden Shakespeare as the protagonist, if the comedy were from the pen of her delightful boy, Will. Had tea been known in Shakespeare's time, how much more closely he would have brought his sexes under one roof instead of sending the more animal of the two off to The Boar's Head and The Mermaid, leaving the ladies to their own verbal devices.

Shakespeare, being such a delicate, as well as virile, poet, would have taken to tea as naturally as a bee takes to a rose or honeysuckle; for the very word *tea* suggests all that is fragrant, and clean, and spotless: linen, silver, china, toast, butter, a charming room with charming women, charmingly gowned; peach and plum and apple trees, with the scent of roses, just beyond the open, half-curtained windows, looking down upon or over orchard or garden, as the May or June morning breezes suggest eternal youth, as they fill the room with perfume, tenderness, love, optimism, and hope in immortality.

Coffee suggests taverns, cafes, sailing vessels, yachts, boardinghouses by the riverside, and pessimism. Tea suggests optimism. Coffee is a tonic; tea, a comfort. Coffee is prose; tea is poetry. Whoever thinks of taking coffee into a sickroom? Who doesn't think of taking in the comforting cup of tea? Can the most vivid imagination picture the angels above the stars drinking coffee? No. Yet, if I were to show them to you over the teacups you would not be surprised or shocked. Would you? Not a bit of it. You would say: "That's a very pretty picture. Pray, what are they talking about, or of whom are they talking?"

Why, of their loved ones below, and of the days of their coming above the stars. They know when to look for us and while the time may seem long to us before the celestial reunion, to them it is short. They do not worry as we do. We could not match their beautiful serenity if we tried, for they know the folly of wishing to break or change divine laws.

What delightful scandals have been born at tea tables—rose and lavender and old point lace scandals: surely, no brutal scandals or treasons, as in the tavern. Tea table gossip surely never seriously hurt a reputation. Well, name one. No? Well, think of the shattered reputations that have fallen around the bottle. Men are the worst gossips unhanged, not women.

In 1652, tea sold for as high as £10 in the leaf. Pepys had his first cup of tea in September 1660. (See his diary.) The rare recipe for making tea in those days was known only to the elect, and here it is:

> **"To a pint of tea, add the yolks of two fresh eggs; then beat them up with as much fine sugar as is sufficient to sweeten the tea, and stir well together. The water must remain no longer upon the tea than while you can chant the Miserere psalm in a leisurely fashion."**

But I am not endorsing recipes of 250 odd years ago. The above is from the knowledge box of a Chinese priest, or a priest from China, called Pere Couplet (don't print it *Quatrain*) in 1667. He gave it to the Earl of Clarendon, and I extend it to you, if you wish to try it.

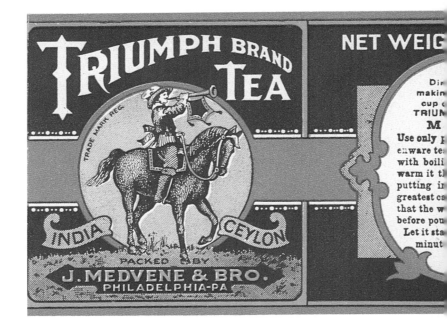

John Milton knew the delights of tea. He drank coffee during the composition of *Paradise Lost* and tea during the building of *Paradise Regained*.

Like all good things, animate and inanimate, tea did not become popular without a struggle. It, like the gradual oak, met with many kinds of opposition from the timid, the prejudiced, and the selfish. All sorts of herbs were put upon the market to offset its popularity such as onions, sage, marjoram, the Arctic bramble, the sloe, goat-weed, Mexican goosefoot, speedwell, wild geranium, veronica, wormwood, juniper, saffron, carduus benedictus, trefoil, woodsorrel, pepper, mace, scurry grass, plantain, and betony.

Sir Hans Sloane invented herb tea, and Captain Cook's companion, Dr. Solander, invented another tea but it was no use—tea had come to stay, and a blessing it has been to the world when moderately used. You don't want to become a tea drunkard, like Dr. Johnson, nor a coffee fiend, like Balzac. Be moderate in all things, and you are bound to be happy and live long. Moderation in eating, drinking, loving, hating, smoking, talking, acting, fighting, sleeping, walking, lending, borrowing, reading newspapers—in expressing opinions—even in bathing and praying means long life and happiness.

The
Wit,
Wisdom, and
Humor of
Tea

ea tempers the spirits and harmonizes the mind, dispels lassitude and relieves fatigue, awakens thought and prevents drowsiness, lightens or refreshes the body, and clears the perceptive faculties.

Confucius

CLEAN GLASS WITH SAPOLIO.

DONALDSON BROTHERS, N.Y.

Thank God for tea! What would the world do without tea? How did it exist? I am glad I was not born before tea.

Sydney Smith

"Sammy," whispered Mr. Weller, "if some o' these here people don't want tappin' to-morrow mornin', I ain't your father, and that's wot it is. Why this here old lady next me is a drownin' herself in tea."

"Be quiet, can't you?" murmured Sam.

"Sam," whispered Mr. Weller a moment afterward, in a tone of deep agitation, "mark my words, my boy; if that 'ere secretary feller keeps on for five minutes more, he'll blow himself up with toast and water."

"Well, let him if he likes," replied Sam, "it ain't no bis'ness of yourn."

"If this here lasts much longer, Sammy," said Mr. Weller, in the same low voice, "I shall feel it my duty as a human bein' to rise and address the cheer. There's a young 'ooman on the next form but two, as has drank nine breakfast cups and a half, and she's a swellin' wisibly before my wery eyes."

PICKWICK PAPERS, *Charles Dickens*

Books upon books have been published in relation to the evil effects of tea drinking, but for all that, no statistics are at hand to show that their arguments have made teetotalers of tea drinkers. One of the best things, however, said against tea drinking is distinctly in its favor to a certain extent. It is from one Dr. Paulli, who laments that "tea so dries the bodies of the Chinese that they can hardly spit." This will find few sympathizers among us. We suggest the quotation to some enterprising tea dealer to be used in a streetcar advertisement.

Of all methods of making tea, the one that was hit upon by Heine's Italian landlord was perhaps the most economical. Heine lodged in a house

at Lucca, the first floor of which was occupied by an English family. The latter complained of the cookery of Italy in general, and their landlord's in particular. Heine declared the landlord brewed the best tea he had ever tasted in the country, and to convince his doubtful English friends invited them to take tea with him and his brother. The invitation was accepted. Tea time came, but no tea. When the poet's patience was exhausted, his brother went to the kitchen to expedite matters. There he found his landlord, who, in blissfull ignorance of what company the Heines had invited, cried: "You can get no tea, for the family on the first floor have not taken tea this evening."

The tea that had delighted Heine was made from the used leaves of the English party, who found and made their own tea, and thus afforded the landlord an opportunity of obtaining at once praise and profit by this Italian method of serving a pot of tea.

CHAMBERS' JOURNAL

FATE

Matrons who toss the cup, and see
The grounds of Fate in grounds of tea.
                    —*Churchill.*

In spite of the fact that coffee is just as important a beverage as tea, tea has been sipped more in literature.

Tea is certainly as much of a social drink as coffee, and more domestic, for the reason that the teacup hours are the family hours. As these are the hours when the sexes are thrown together, and as most of the poetry and philosophy of tea drinking teem with female virtues, vanities, and whimsicalities, the inference is that, without women, tea would be nothing; and without tea, women would be stale, flat, and uninteresting. With them it is a polite, purring, soft, gentle, kind, sympathetic, delicious beverage.

In support of this theory, notice what Pope, Gay, Crabbe, Cowper, Dryden, and others have written on the subject.

> **The tea-cup time of hood and hoop,**
> **And when the patch was worn**

wrote Tennyson of the early half of the seventeenth century.

What a suggestive couplet, full of the foibles and follies of the times! A picture a la mode of the period when fair dames made their red cheeks cute with eccentric patches. Ornamented with high coiffures, powdered hair, robed in satin petticoats and square-cut bodices, they blossomed, according to the old engravings, into most fetching figures. Even the beaux of the day affected feminine frills in their many-colored, bell-skirted waistcoats, lace ruffles, patches, and powdered queues.

Dryden must have succumbed to the charms of women through tea when he wrote:

> **And thou, great Anna, whom three realms obey,**
> **Dost sometimes take councel, and sometimes tay.**

From the great vogue which tea started grew a taste for china; the more peculiar and striking the design, the more valuable the teaset. Pope in one of his satirical compositions praises the composure of a woman who is

> **Mistress of herself though china fall.**

Even that fine old bachelor, philosopher, and humorist Charles Lamb thought that the subject deserved an essay. In speaking of the ornaments on the teacup he says, in *Old China:*

> **I like to see my old friends, whom distance cannot diminish, figuring up in the air (so they appear to our optics), yet on terra firma still, for so we must in courtesy interpret that speck of deeper blue which the decorous artist, to prevent absurdity, has made to spring up beneath their sandals. I love the men with women's faces and the women, if possible, with still more womanish expressions.**

Lady Purr-Kins Tea Party.

Here is a young and courtly Mandarin handing tea to a lady from a salver—two miles off. See how distance seems to set off respect! And here the same lady, or another—for likeness is identity on tea-cups—is stepping into a little fairy boat, moored on the hither side of this calm garden river. She is stepping with a dainty, mincing foot, at right angle of incidence (as angles go in our world) that must infallibly land her in the midst of a flowery mead—a furlong off on the other side of the same strange stream!

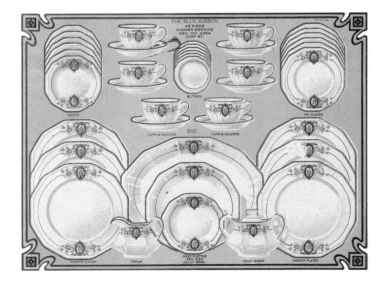

The *Spectator* and the *Tatler* were also susceptible to the female influence that tea inspired. In both of these journals there are frequent allusions to teaparties and china. At these gatherings, poets and dilettante literary gentlemen read their verses and essays to the ladies, who criticized their merits. These "literary teas" became so contagious that a burning desire for authorship took possession of the ladies, for among those who made their debut as authors about this time were Fanny Burney, Mrs. Alphra Behn, Mrs. Manley, the Countess of Winchelsea, and a host of others.

One of the readers of the *Spectator* wrote as follows:

> "**Mr. Spectator:** **Your paper is a part of my tea equipage, and my servant knows my humor so well that, calling for my breakfast this morning (it being past my usual hour), she answered the *Spectator* was not come in, but that the teakettle boiled, and she expected it every minute.**"

Crabbe, too, was a devotee of ladies, literature, and tea, for he wrote

> **The gentle fair on nervous tea relies,**
> **Whilst gay good-nature sparkles in her eyes;**
> **And inoffensive scandal fluttering round,**
> **Too rough to tickle and too light to wound.**

What better proof do we want, therefore, that to women's influence is due the cultivation and retention of the tea habit? Without tea, what would become of women, and without women and tea, what would become of our domestic literary men and matinee idols? They would not sit at home or in salons and write and act things. There would be no homes to sit in, no salons or theatres to act in, and dramatic art would receive a blow from which it could not recover in a century, at least.

hat would women novelists do without tea in their books? The novelists of the rougher sex write of "over the coffee and cigars"; or, "around the gay and festive board"; or, "over a bottle of old port"; or, "another bottle of dry and sparkling champagne was cracked"; or, "and the succulent Welsh rarebits were washed down with royal mugs of musty ale"; or, "as the storm grew fiercer, the captain ordered all hands to splice the main brace, to take a drink of rum." Or

men might write "as he gulped down the last drink of fiery whiskey, he reeled through the tavern door, and his swaying form drifted into the bleak, black night as a roar of laughter drowned his repentant sobs." But the ladies of the novel confine themselves almost exclusively to tea, rarely allowing their heroes and heroines to indulge in even coffee, though they sometimes treat their heroes to wine; but their heroines rarely get anything from them but Oolong.

Tea-Table Verses

In the year 1700, J. Roberts, a London publisher, issued a pamphlet of about fifty pages which was made up as follows:

Poem upon Tea in Two Cantos	34	pages
Dedication of the poem	6	"
Preface to the poem	2	"
Poem upon the poem	1	"
Introduction to the poem	4	"
To the author upon the poem	1	"
Postscript	3	"
Tea-Table	2	"

The poem—the pièce de résistance—which is by one Nahum Tate, who figures on the title page as "Servant to His Majesty," is an allegory; and although good in spots, it is too long and too dry to reproduce here. The "Tea-Table" verses however will be found interesting and entertaining.

THE FORTUNE-TELLER.

WHAT DOES THIS LOVELY MAIDEN SEE ?   AND HER'S GOOD FORTUNE E'ER MUST BE -
HER FORTUNE IN A CUP OF TEA,   ❋   SHE BUYS THE "GREAT AMERICAN" TEA.

Tea Table

Hail, Queen of Plants, Pride of Elysian Bow'rs!
How shall we speak thy complicated Pow'rs?
Thou Won'drous Panacea to assuage
The Calentures of Youths' fermenting rage,
And Animate the freezing Veins of age.

To Bacchus when our Griefs repair for Ease,
The Remedy proves worse than the Disease.
Where Reason we must lose to keep the Round,
And drinking others' Healths, our own confound:
Whilst Tea, our Sorrows to beguile,
Sobriety and Mirth does reconcile:
For to this Nectar we the Blessing owe,
To grow more Wise, as we more Cheerful grow.

Whilst fancy does her brightest beams dispense,
And decent Wit diverts without Offense.
Then in Discourse of Nature's mystick Pow'rs
And Noblest Themes, we pass the well spent Hours.
Whilst all around the Virtues' Sacred Band,
And list'ning Graces, pleas'd Attendants, stand.

Thus our Tea-Conversation we employ,
Where with Delight, Instruction we enjoy;
Quaffing, without the waste of Time or Wealth,
The Sov'reign Drink of Pleasure and of Health.

The
Making and
Taking of Tea
in Other
Lands

The queen of teas in Japan is a fine straw-colored beverage, delicate and subtle in flavor, and as invigorating as a glass of champagne. It is real Japan tea, and seldom leaves its native heath for the reason that, while it is peculiarly adaptable to the Japanese constitution, it is too stimulating for finely tuned and oversensitive Americans who, by the way, are said to be the largest customers for Japan teas of other grades in the world.

This particular tea, which looks as harmless as our own importations of the leaf, is a very insidious beverage, as an American lady soon found out after taking some of it late at night. She declared, after drinking a small cup before retiring, she did not close her eyes in sleep for a week. We do not know the name of the brand of tea, and are glad of it; for we live in a section where the women are especially curious.

But the drink of the people at large in Japan is green tea, although powdered tea is also used, but reserved for special functions and ceremonial occasions. Tea, over there, is not made by infusing the leaves with boiling water, as is the case with us; but the boiling water is first carefully cooled in another vessel to 176 degrees Fahrenheit. The leaves are also renewed for every infusion. It would be crime against his August Majesty, the Palate, to use the same leaves more than once in Japan. The preparation of good tea is regarded by the Japanese as the height of social art, and for that reason it is an important element in the domestic, diplomatic, political, and general life of the country.

Tea is the beverage—the masterpiece of every meal, even if it be nothing but boiled rice. Every artisan and laborer going to work carries with him his rice-box of lacquered wood, a kettle, a tea caddy, a teapot, a cup, and his chopsticks. Milk and sugar are generally eschewed. The Japanese and the Chinese never indulge in either of these ingredients in tea; the use of which, they claim, spoils the delicate aroma.

It is the custom in both Japan and China to offer tea to every visitor upon his arrival. Not to do this would be an unpardonable breach of national manners. Even in the shops, the customer is regaled with a soothing cup before the goods are displayed to him. This does not, however, impose any

This Booklet is issued by the American Japanese Tea Committee to advertise and furnish correct information concerning Japan Tea, from its mythical origin up to the present day.

" Thank God for tea! What would the world do without tea ? —how did it exist ? I am glad I was not born before tea."
Rev. Sydney Smith

No normal person was ever injured by drinking Japan tea; there is no record of such a case even when taken to excess.

obligation on the prospective purchaser, but it is, nevertheless, a good stimulant to part with his money. This appears to be a very ancient tradition in China and Japan—so ancient that it is continued by the powers that be in Paradise and Hades according to a translation called *Strange Stories from My Small Library*, a classical Chinese work published in 1679.

The old domestic etiquette of Japan never intrusted to a servant the making of tea for a guest. It was made by the master of the house himself; the custom probably growing out of the innate politeness and courtesy of a people who believe that an honored visitor is entitled to the best entertainment possible to give him.

As soon as a guest is seated upon his mat, a small tray is set before the master of the house. Upon this tray is a tiny teapot with a handle at right angles to the spout. Other parts of this outfit include a highly artistic teakettle

THE TEA CEREMONY

The famous Tea Ceremony, CHA-NO-YU, is a development from ancient days. The rules of CHA-NO-YU, as observed in modern Japan, were drawn up several hundred years ago. They prescribe in extreme detail the conduct of the ceremony. The tea-room must be exactly ten feet square, entered from a specially designed garden by a door only three feet high, and utensils in size and decoration must be in accord with the requirements of the CHA-NO-YU code.

A little powdered tea, called Matsucha, is placed in a tea bowl. A dipper of boiling water is added, and the infusion whipped to a froth with a bamboo whisk.

The guests kneel about on mats, dignified, placid, as becomes those who strictly commune on the high destiny of Man in the Universe. Every movement is studied and deliberate. With great solemnity they receive the bowl and sip reflectively the delicate liquor which we know as the "Champagne of Teas."

DINING WHILE SEATED ON THE MATS

In Japan the guests invariably finish the banquet with a few cups of mild Japan Tea. It aids digestion and moderates that heavy feeling due to dining too well.

No function of this kind is complete unless it begins and is finished up with tea.

filled with hot water, and a requisite number of small cups, set in metal or bamboo trays. These trays are used for handing the cups around, but the guest is not expected to take one. The cups being without handles, and not easy to hold, the visitor must therefore be careful lest he let one slip through his untutored fingers.

The teapot is drenched with hot water before the tea is put in; then more hot water is poured over the leaves, and soon poured off into the cups. This is repeated several times, but the hot water is never allowed to stand on the grounds over a minute.

The Japanese all adhere to the general household custom of the country in keeping the necessary tea apparatus in readiness. In the living room of every house is contained a brazier with live coals, a kettle to boil water, a tray with teapot, cups, and a tea caddy.

DIRECTIONS FOR MAKING A PERFECT CUP OF JAPAN GREEN TEA

1. Buy a good grade of Japan Green Tea. One pound will make 250 to 300 cups of moderate strength. The best you can buy will only cost you a fraction of a cent per cup—therefore, there is no real economy in buying cheap tea.
2. An earthen teapot is best and should be scalded before using.
3. Put in a teaspoonful for each cup of tea.
4. Be sure the water is thoroughly boiling before pouring into the teapot.
5. Let the infusion steep three to five minutes before using.
6. Serve with or without lemon, milk or sugar, according to taste.
7. For Iced-Tea, make the tea in the regular way, using double the quantity of tea. Pour off the infusion into another vessel and add ice.

THE CUP THAT CHEERS. "WELCOME" IN JAPAN, THE LAND OF COLOR, COURTESY and CHARM

Their neighbors, the Chinese, are just as alert; for no matter what hour of the day it may be, they always keep a kettle of boiling water over the hot coals, ready to make and serve the beverage at a moment's notice. No visitor is allowed to leave without being offered a cup of their tea, and they themselves are glad to share in their own hospitality.

The Chinese use boiling water, and pour it upon the dry tea in each cup. A cup is often shaped like a small bowl, with a saucer a little less in diameter than the top of the bowl. This saucer also serves another purpose, and is often used for a cover when the tea is making. After the boiling water is poured upon the tea, it is covered for a couple of minutes, until the leaves have separated and fallen to the bottom of the cup. This process renders the tea clear, delightfully fragrant, and appetizing.

A variety of other cups are also used, the most prominent being without

DISTRIBUTION OF JAPAN GREEN TEA

Japan produces approximately 100 million pounds of tea, over three quarters being used for native consumption. The United States early recognized the merit of Japan Green Tea, and today some 18 million pounds are annually used—equal to approximately five billion cups.

Canada consumes about 3 million pounds, and in the past five years, Japan Tea has met with favor in Russia which now imports 1,500,000 pounds, and the trade is steadily growing.

STEAMER LOADING

Loading Japan Tea in Shimidzu Harbor at the foot of Great Fuji Mountain.

handles, one or two sizes larger than the Japanese. They are made of the finest china, set in silver trays beautifully wrought, ornate in treatment and design.

A complete tea outfit is a part of the outfitting of every *Ju-bako*, "picnic-box," which every Japanese is provided when on a journey, making an excursion, or attending a picnic. The Japanese are very much given to these out-of-door affairs, which they call *Hanami*—"looking at the flowers." No wonder they are fond of these pleasures, for it is a land of lovely landscapes and heaven-sent airs, completely in harmony with the poetic and artistic natures of this splendid people.

Teahouses—*Châ*—which take the place of our cafes and barrooms, but which, nevertheless, serve a far higher social purpose, are everywhere in evidence: on the highroads and byroads, tucked away in templed groves and public resorts of every nature.

Among the Japanese are a number of ceremonial, social, and literary tea parties which reflect their courtly and chivalrous spirit, and keep alive the traditions of the people more, perhaps, than any other of their functions.

The most important of these tea parties are exclusively for gentlemen, and their forms and ceremonies rank among the most refined usages of polite society. The customs of these gatherings are so peculiarly characteristic of the Japanese that few foreign observers have an opportunity of attending them. These are the tea parties of a semiliterary or aesthetic character, and the ceremonious *Châ-no-ya*. In the first prevails the easy and unaffected tone of the well-bred gentleman. In the other are observed the strictest rules of etiquette both in speech and behavior. But the former entertainment is by far the most interesting. The Japanese love and taste for fine scenery is shown in the settings and surroundings. To this picturesque outlook, recitals of romance and impromptu poetry add intellectual charm to the tea party.

For these occasions the host selects a teahouse located in well-laid-out grounds and commanding a fine view. In this he lays mats equal to the number of guests. By sliding the partition and removing the front wall the place is transformed into an open hall overlooking the landscape. The room is filled with choice flowers, and the art treasures of the host which at other times are stored away in the fireproof vault, or "go down," of his private residence—contribute artistic beauty and decoration to the scene. Folding screens and hanging pictures painted by celebrated artists, costly lacquer-ware, bronze, china, and other heirlooms are tastefully distributed about the room.

Stories told at these tea parties are called by the Japanese names of *Châ-banashi,* meaning "tea stories," or *Hiti-Kucha,* "one-month stories," short stories told at one sitting. At times professional storytellers are employed. Of these there are two kinds: storytellers and "crossroad tradition narrators," both of whom since olden times have been the faithful custodians and disseminators of native folklore and tales.

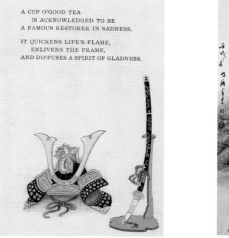

A CUP O'GOOD TEA
IS ACKNOWLEDGED TO BE
A FAMOUS RESTORER IN SADNESS.

IT QUICKENS LIFE'S FLAME,
ENLIVENS THE FRAME,
AND DIFFUSES A SPIRIT OF GLADNESS.

TRANSLATION OF JAPANESE CHARACTER
"TEA"; the soil where the Tea plant grows is
sacred; if a man drinks tea, he enjoys longevity.

The Chinese teahouses and similar resorts are just as numerous and popular as they are in the neighboring country. Perhaps the most interesting caterers in China, however, are the coolies, who sell hot water in the rural districts. These itinerants have an ingenious way of announcing their coming by a whistling kettle. This vessel contains a compartment for fire with a funnel going through the top. A coin with a hole is placed so that when the water is boiling a regular steam whistle is heard.

Plentiful as tea is in China, however, the poor people there, especially in the northern part of China, are obliged to use the last pickings of tea, commonly known as *brick tea,* which is very poor and coarse in quality. It is pressed into bricks about eight by twelve inches in size, and whenever a quantity of it is needed, a piece is knocked off and pulverized in a kettle of boiling water. Other ingredients, consisting of salt, milk, butter, a little pepper, and vinegar, are added, and this combination constitutes the entire meal of the family.

Tea in China and Japan is the standby of every meal—the never-failing and ever-ready refreshment. Besides being the courteous offering to the visitor, it serves a high purpose in the home life of these peoples, uniting the family and friends in their domestic life and pleasures at all times and seasons. At home round the brazier and the lamp in winter evenings, at picnic parties and excursions to the shady glen during the fine season, tea is the social connecting medium, the intellectual stimulant, and the universal drink of these far-and-away peoples.

COST OF TEA

When first tea became known and was used in Europe, the cost was very high, sometimes over $10 per pound.

Improved methods have brought prices within every one's means, and it is perhaps the most economical combined food and drink known.

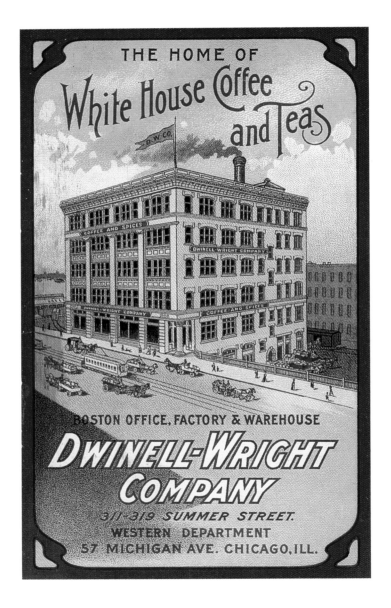

*W*hile tea drinking outside of Japan and China is not attended with any "high days and holidays," still there are countries where it is just as important an element of the daily life of its people.

Among the Burmese, a newly married couple, to insure a happy life, exchange a mixture of tea leaves steeped in oil.

In Bokhara, every man carries a small bag of tea about with him. When he is thirsty he hands a certain quantity over to a booth keeper who makes the beverage for him. The Bokhariot, who is a confirmed tea slave, finds it just as hard to pass a tea booth without indulging in the herb as our own inebriates do to go by a corner cafe. His breakfast beverage is *Schitschaj*—tea in which bread is soaked and flavored with milk, cream, or mutton fat. During the daytime he drinks green tea with cakes of flour and mutton suet. It is considered a gross breach of manners to cool the hot tea by blowing the breath. This is overcome by supporting the right elbow in the left hand and giving an easy, graceful, circular movement to the cup. The time it takes for each kind of tea to draw is calculated to a second. When the can is emptied it is passed around among the company for each tea drinker to take up as many leaves as can be held between the thumb and finger, the leaves being considered a special dainty.

An English traveller once journeying through Asiatic Russia was obliged to claim the hospitality of a family of Buratsky Arabs. At mealtime the mistress of the tent placed a large kettle on the fire, wiped it carefully with a horse's tail, filled it with water, threw in some coarse tea and a little salt. When this was nearly boiled she stirred the mixture with a brass ladle until the liquor became very brown, and she poured it into another vessel. Cleaning the kettle as before, the woman set it again on the fire to fry a paste of meal and fresh butter. Upon this she poured the tea and some thick cream, stirred it, and after a time the whole was taken off the fire and set aside to cool. Half-pint mugs were handed around and the tea ladled into them: the result, a pasty tea forming meat and drink, satisfying both hunger and thirst.

M. Vámbéry says: "The picture of a newly encamped caravan in the summer months on the steppes of Central Asia is a truly interesting one. While the camels in the distance, but still in sight, graze greedily or crush the juicy thistles, the travellers, even to the poorest among them, sit with their teacups in their hands and eagerly sip the costly beverage. It is nothing more than a greenish warm water, innocent of sugar and often decidedly turbid; still, human art has discovered no food, invented no nectar, which is so grateful, so refreshing in the desert as this unpretending drink. I have still a vivid recollection of its wonderful effects. As I sipped the first drops, a soft fire filled my veins, a fire which enlivened without intoxicating. The later draughts affected both heart and head; the eye became peculiarly bright and began to glow. In such moments I felt an indescribable rapture and sense of comfort. My companions sunk in sleep; I could keep myself awake and dream with open eyes!"

Tea is the national drink of Russia, and as indispensable an ingredient of the table there as bread or meat. It is taken at all hours of the day and

night, and in all the griefs of the Russian he flies to tea for mental refuge and consolation. Tea is drunk out of tumblers in Russia. In the homes of the wealthy these tumblers are held in silver holders like the sockets that hold our soda water glasses.

In every Russian town teahouses flourish. In these public resorts a large glass of tea with plenty of sugar in it is served at what would cost, in our money, about two cents. Tea with lemon is so general that milk with the drink, over there, is considered a fad. Some in Russia take a lump of sugar in their mouths and let the tea trickle through it. Travelling tea peddlers, equipped with kettles wrapped up in towels to preserve the heat, and a row of glasses in leather pockets, furnish a glass of hot tea at any hour of the day or night.

The Russian samovar—from the Greek "to boil"—itself is a graceful dome-topped brass urn with a cylinder two or three inches in diameter passing through it from top to bottom. The cylinder is filled with live coals and keeps the water boiling hot. The Russian teapots are porcelain or earthen.

Hot water to heat the pot is first put in and then poured out; dry tea is then put in and boiling water poured over it, after which the pot is placed on top of the samovar.

We all know about tea drinking in England. To the traditional Englishman's mind it means simply a quiet evening at home, attended by the papers and serious conversations in which the head of the house deals out political and domestic wisdom until ten o'clock. During the day, tea taking begins with breakfast and rounds up on the fashionable thoroughfares in the afternoon. These places arecalled tea shops, and in them one may acquire the latest handshake, the freshest tea and gossip, see the newest modes and millinery, meet and greet the whirl of the world. An interesting study of types, in contrasts and conditions of society, worth the price of a whole chest of choice tea.

We are pretty prosaic tea drinkers in America. Is it because there is not enough "touch and go" about the drink, or that we are too busy to settle

down to the quiet, comfort, and thoughtful tea ways of
our contemporaries? Wait until a few things are settled;
when our kitchen queens do not leave us in the "gray of
the morning," and all of our daughters have obtained
diplomas in the art and science of gastronomy.

However made or taken, tea at best or worst is
a glorious drink. As a stimulant for the tired traveller
and weary worker it is unique in its rest-
ful, retiring, soothing, and
caressing qualities.

In the interior of Australia all the men drink tea. They drink it all day long and in quantities and at a strength that would seem to be poisonous. On Sunday morning the teamaker starts with a clean pot and a clean record. The pot is hung over the fire with a sufficiency of water in it for the day's brew, and when this has boiled he pours into it enough of the fragrant herb to produce a deep, coffee-colored liquid.

On Monday, without removing yesterday's tea leaves, he repeats the process; on Tuesday da capo, and on Wednesday da capo, and so on through the week. Toward the close of it the great pot is filled with an acrid mash of tea leaves, out of which the liquor is squeezed by the pressure of a tin cup.

By this time the tea is of the color of rusty iron, incredibly bitter and disagreeable to the uneducated palate. The native calls it "real good old post and rails," the simile being obviously drawn from a stiff and dangerous jump, and regards it as having been brought to perfection.

Five O'Clock Tea

here is a fallacy among certain tea fanciers that the origin of five o'clock tea was due to hygienic demand. These students of the stomach contend that as a tonic and gentle stimulant, when not taken with meat, it is not to be equalled. With meat or any but light food it is considered harmful. Taken between luncheon and dinner it drives away fatigue and acts as a tonic. This is good if true, but it is only a theory, after all. Our theory is that five o'clock in the afternoon is the ladies' leisure hour, and that the taking of tea at that time is an escape from *ennui*.

Sydney Smith

One evening when Sydney Smith was drinking tea with Mrs. Austin, the servant entered the crowded room with a boiling teakettle in his hand. It seemed doubtful, nay, impossible, he should make his way among the numerous gossips. But on the first approach of the steaming kettle the crowd receded on all sides, Mr. Smith among the rest, though carefully watching the progress of the lad to the table.

"I declare," said he, addressing Mrs. Austin, "a man who wishes to make his way in life could do no better than go through the world with a boiling teakettle in his hand."

Life of Rev. Sydney Smith

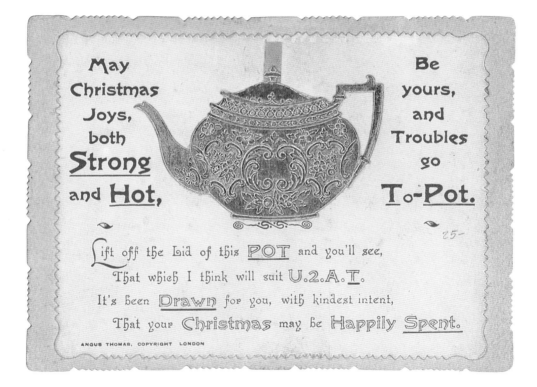

May
Christmas
Joys,
both
Strong
and **Hot,**

Be
yours,
and
Troubles
go

To-Pot.

Lift off the Lid of this <u>POT</u> and you'll see,

That which I think will suit U.2.A.<u>T</u>.

It's been <u>Drawn</u> for you, with kindest intent,

That your Christmas may be Happily <u>Spent</u>.

The good doctor evidently lived up to his reputation as a tea drinker at all times and places. Cumberland, the dramatist, in his memoirs gives a story illustrative of the doctor's tea-drinking powers: "I remember when Sir Joshua Reynolds, at my home, reminded Dr. Johnson that he had drunk eleven cups of tea. 'Sir,' he replied, 'I did not count your glasses of wine; why should you number my cups of tea?"

At another time a certain Lady Macleod, after pouring out sixteen cups for him, ventured mildly to ask whether a basin would not save him trouble and be more convenient. "I wonder, madam," he replied, roughly, "why all ladies ask such questions?"

"It is to save yourself trouble, not me," was the tactful answer of his hostess.

Boswell and Johnson at the Mitre.

A Cup of Tea

From St. Nicholas, *December 1899:*

Now Grietje from her window sees the leafless poplars lean
Against a windy sunset sky with streaks of golden green;
The still canal is touched with light from that wild, wintry sky,
And, dark and gaunt, the windmill flings its bony arms on high.
"It's growing late; it's growing cold; I'm all alone," says she;
"I'll put the little kettle on, to make a cup of tea!"

Mild radiance from the porcelain stove reflects on shining tiles;
The kettle beams, so red and bright that Grietje thinks it smiles;
The kettle sings—so soft and low it seems as in a dream—
The song that's like a lullaby, the pleasant song of steam;
"The summer's gone; the storks are flown; I'm always here, you see,
To sing and sing, and shine and shine, and make a cup of tea!"

The blue delft plates and dishes gleam, all ranged upon the shelf;
The tall Dutch clock tick-ticks away, just talking to itself;
The brindled pussy cuddles down, and basks and blinks and purrs;
And rosy, sleepy Grietje droops that snow-white cap of hers.
"I do like winter after all; I'm very glad," says she,
"I put-my-little-kettle-on-to make-a cup-of-tea!"

Helen Gray Cone